June Sarpong MBE is one of the most recognizable British television presenters and broadcasters and the co-founder of the WIE Network (Women: Inspiration and Enterprise). She is the author of *Diversify*, an empowering guide to why a more open society means a more successful one, which won the 2018 London's Big Read award.

The Power of Women

June Sarpong MBE

ONE PLACE. MANY STORIES

HQ
An imprint of HarperCollins*Publishers* Ltd
1 London Bridge Street
London SE1 9GF

This edition 2018

1

First published in Great Britain by
HQ, an imprint of HarperCollins*Publishers* Ltd 2018

A catalogue record for this book is
available from the British Library.

ISBN: 978-0-00-830676-2

Typeset by Palimpsest Book Production Ltd, Falkirk, Stirlingshire
Printed and bound in Great Britain by
CPI Group (UK) Ltd, Croydon, CR0 4YY

MIX
Paper from
responsible sources
FSC™ C007454

This book is produced from independently certified FSC™ paper
to ensure responsible forest management.

For more information visit: www.harpercollins.co.uk/green

To every woman trying to be her best
self, and every man trying to help.

INTRODUCTION:

THE EMPOWERED WOMAN

Feminism (n). The advocacy of women's rights on the ground of the equality of the sexes.
                                        Oxford English Dictionary

The definition and the focus of feminism has changed through the ages as it has sought to resist and overcome the tenets of patriarchy. Women have always fought for their place within the household or family, usually employing femininity as an iron fist in velvet gloves, using covert or non-confrontational means to assert themselves. The political, social, and cultural upheavals of the twentieth century gave women a greater aware-ness of mass movements demanding political and social change. Women also became organized, but with a different end goal to many of the radical movements that sought the overthrow of the existing order.

The women's movement – feminism – did not want to take power, but to share in it. However, the competitiveness which society often instils in men means some see the pursuit of power as a zero-sum game. This has resulted in any challenge to the status quo often prompting fear and suspicion – to the extent that feminism has frequently been met with aggression and violence, both from the state and individual males.

Thankfully, both men and women have evolved to the extent that the majority of us acknowledge that there needs to be gender equality, and politicians (still mainly men) have passed laws to underpin this belief. However, the zero-sum mentality still exists, where men view feminism as a movement of confrontation rather than an opportunity to achieve solutions to inequality. Some women also shy away from the label of feminism as it can often be typecast as a movement with unreasonable demands, that victimizes and takes power from men in favour of a female hierarchy.

True feminism is nothing of the sort. Rather, it is a movement that seeks to create the equal balance between the genders that we all need, defined in the *Oxford English Dictionary* as 'The advocacy of women's rights on the ground of the equality of the sexes.' We seem to get fixated on the advocacy of women's rights over the aim – which is *equality*.

Neither men nor women need to be afraid of the term feminism, because the imbalance and inequality that requires its existence costs us all dearly. Gender imbalance and inequality in female education will impact the male and female children who women might give birth to. Gender imbalance or inequality at work and in business impacts on how effectively a business or organisation is able to operate. These are issues that concern us all regardless of gender, which is why we must act on Chimamanda Ngozi Adichie's clarion call. Indeed: *We Should All Be Feminists.*

As we celebrate the centenary of female suffrage in the UK, in the wake of the explosion of the #MeToo and #TimesUp movements and calls for greater pay transparency, it's clear from recent indicators that there is a fierce appetite for a change in the way society treats women. With this glorious uprising of women everywhere we could be forgiven for feeling a sense of achievement, and indeed the social and cultural change in Western society has been significant and has ushered in a redefining of assumed gender relations at work and elsewhere. But the call for gender equality is nothing new and there is still much work to be done.

Women are the largest oppressed group in the world, and the degrees of subjugation vary from country to country, with women in the West faring much better than their counterparts in developing parts of the world. But even in the UK and the US, **there are more women living in poverty than men**[1], and of the people who were paid *below* the National Living Wage in 2016, 64% were women[2]. *Levelling* the playing field will be a struggle but it will, without question, be worth it for everyone, given the rewards that are to be won. According to the UK version of the McKinsey Global Institute's Power of Parity report, **bridging the UK gender gap at work 'has the potential to create an extra £150 billion on top of business-as-usual GDP forecasts in 2025, and could translate into 840,000 additional female employees'**.[3] Certainly, as things stand, we are often failing to harness the full potential of 50 per cent of society. Imagine the technological, cultural, and political progress we could make if we fully empowered that half of society.

It can be tempting to see this as exclusively a women's issue. But that's not the case. And in addition to discussing how important it is that we provide a level playing field for mothers, daughters, sisters, and friends, this book will prove just how much society as a whole – including husbands, sons, brothers and male friends

– has to gain, economically and socially, from the rise of empowered women.

And there are wider benefits too. Women are usually the *de facto* operational managers of a home. An ability to manage a budget, resolve conflict, and inspire excellence come as standard. This skill set is an obvious advantage in management and should not be overlooked or undermined. That is not to say these attributes are exclusive to women, but those who are able to demonstrate these transferable skills are undoubtedly an asset to any business. For the male boss above her this operational manager brings a responsible pair of hands, and for the male subordinate, possibly an encouraging style of leadership that fosters progression and development. And for colleagues – yes, an element of competition, but also an opportunity to learn alternative styles of working and thinking. Women have shaped the template and culture of the home for centuries; it's now time for us to add a lasting 'feminine' dynamic to the workplace, and reap the social and economic benefits of doing so.

The results – personal, cultural, and economic – of gender equality will be spectacularly beneficial, for women, for men, and for society as a whole. But we won't get there unless we can convince even the biggest cynics that feminism works for everyone. This book will highlight women's lost potential and, more importantly, provide the tools and arguments to support the fact that gender equality will enable a bright future we will *all* benefit from.

Power in the Media

Throughout the ages, from paintings through to magazine covers and the movies, society's beauty standards have been represented in the media via images that have been heralded as the 'ideal' of the day. Women in particular have been subjected to this relentless objectification and anyone falling short of these standards is either denigrated or ignored, leaving millions of young girls and women feeling unworthy, unrepresented, and fearful of rejection.

Women are held to an entirely different set of standards than their male counterparts – we are valued by the way we look and how young we are; the 'prettier' and younger the better: **only 18 per cent of TV broadcasters over fifty years old are women,[1] and the majority of female film characters are in their twenties [32 per cent] and thirties [25 per cent][2]**. The mental pressure this creates wreaks havoc on our self-esteem. As a result, women are plagued with a level of self-doubt and self-criticism (myself included) that men do not have to face. And it's led to a narrow representation of women, not just in the visible media but behind the scenes as well.

As someone who has worked in the media for almost twenty years, I am very much aware of the power of the visual image and the impact it has on how we value ourselves; I've experienced its discriminating effects first-hand. With ordinary women drastically under-represented, the proliferation of misogynistic trolling on social media, and the easy access to online porn, it's become blindingly obvious that unrealistic, unrepresentative, and sometimes unhealthy images of women are projected into people's homes and minds on a daily basis. To counter this, we clearly need our media to start involving and portraying women in a more balanced and affirming manner.

The Oscar-winning actress Geena Davis has become a leading advocate for the better representation of women in the media: her Institute on Gender in Media is doing a stellar job of holding Hollywood accountable by monitoring the representation of women both in front of and behind the camera. I was fortunate enough to discuss this issue in detail with Geena when she delivered the keynote address at the Women: Inspiration and Enterprise (WIE) New York 2012 conference, which I helped to organize. And, in the six years since Geena delivered her keynote not much has changed – the data from her latest research on gender equality in advertising is quite startling: when studying the screen- and speaking-time of women in commercials (across 5 English-speaking territories), **there had been no discernible change in a decade. In 2006, 43.6 per cent of all commercials showed women on screen for 20 per cent or less of the commercial. By 2016, the figure was a similar 44.2 per cent. Commercials with men only were five times as common as women-only adverts (despite the fact that women dominate in many purchasing decisions). In advertising, men were on screen about four times as much as women.**[3]

We see a similar picture in TV and film, where **of the 100 highest-grossing films of 2017, women represented: 8 per cent of directors, 10 per cent of writers, 2 per cent of cinematographers, 24 per cent of producers, and 14 per cent of editors.**[4]

The Institute's findings point to a systemic problem at the very core of the industry: the largely male decision makers in the commissioning meetings, and maybe even the writers and directors themselves, are unwilling to put women at the heart of their stories. Geena is very frank about the problem: 'All of Hollywood is run on one assumption: that women will watch stories about men, but men won't watch stories about women. It is a horrible indictment of our society if we assume that one half of our population is just not interested in the other half.'[5]

In some ways, we are trapped in a vicious circle here. Boys see from early on that male superheroes have a wide range of abilities, but the female's superpower will primarily be that she looks good in a tight outfit that may well be nice to look at, but it can't be called *interesting*. In a world where women on screen are idolized primarily for their appearance and rarely given stories of depth or complexity, it's no wonder that it's been hardwired into all of society that women are not interesting to men.

But things are beginning to change, and savvy studios are reaping the rewards. **In 2017, the three highest-grossing films of the year in the US all had female leads:** *Star Wars – The Last Jedi* (Daisy Ridley), *Beauty and the Beast* (Emma Watson) and *Wonder Woman* (Gal Gadot).[6]

Women need the support of men to create new, more inclusive stories, because of course part of the issue is undoubtedly that the decision makers, writers, and directors are – as the stats above confirm – also predominantly men. But we all need to challenge our internalized misogyny. Gender discrimination can be insidious and more difficult to detect because it doesn't carry the same level of self-reproach as racial or disability discrimination. The vast majority inherently know racial discrimination is wrong, even if we carry conscious or unconscious bias, but with gender our ideas about what constitutes sexism are warped, so diagnosing misogynistic behaviour can be difficult and confusing.

The challenge, therefore, is manifold. As well as conducting some self-analysis of our own internalized misogyny, we also need to work together to create stories around women, and to make sure women have the opportunity to tell those stories themselves. Until women see more balanced and inspirational images of themselves, the journey to reach the level of unwavering self-belief required to fulfil our potential will be all the harder. As it stands, only the exceptional can get through. Unfortunately, by the mere definition of the word, most of us are not exceptional.

The film industry is not the only culprit in the media, of course. Unfortunately, a lack of diversity is still very much prevalent in mainstream women's magazines, too. Despite it being a female-centric industry, the images that make it onto the pages of our glossy magazines have long been notoriously homogenous – the women are reliably young, thin, and – more often than not – white.

In the US, Anna Wintour, the legendary former

editor-in-chief of American *Vogue*, has been at the forefront of addressing this. Over the last few years she has broken the mould and produced covers that feature leading women of colour such as Rihanna, Michelle Obama, Serena Williams, Zendaya, and Beyoncé. Franca Sozzani, the late great editor of Italian *Vogue*, also made it her mission to make her pages more inclusive and, as with *Wonder Woman* or the astronomical success of *Black Panther*, the numbers speak for themselves; **the famed 'Black' issue of *Vogue*, which featured the most iconic models of colour, past and present, is to date one of the biggest-selling editions of that magazine.**[7]

Unfortunately, the UK still lags seriously behind on this issue, though there could be sunshine on the horizon as we again turn to *Vogue*. The appointment of Edward Enninful as its first editor of colour (who also happens to be a man) could result in the UK's most trusted and elite fashion bible becoming a publication in which all women can see themselves represented.

So far, this seems to be the case. In his short reign as head of *Vogue*, Enninful has already began a wave of more inclusive editorial and covers, which has not only proved refreshing to a wider consumer base but also incredibly lucrative. Vanessa Kingori the first ever female publisher of *British Vogue* (who also happens to

12

be black) recently announced: 'Total sales are up 7.5 per cent since Edward's first issue and UK newsstands sales have also increased. Total advertising revenue is up too, fuelled by a 26 per cent increase in digital advertising, and the company reports a 1,033 per cent increase in events and special projects revenue.'

And as we saw with *Vogue*'s 'Black' issue, or indeed Nike's #betterforit campaign, if done right, inclusivity can also be very lucrative.

But is it any wonder that representative media is the exception rather than the rule? The less public side of prejudice can be found in the severe under-representation of BAME individuals in the creative industries. We're at risk here of taking steps backwards rather than forwards – the government have cut funding to Creative Access, an organization that has been working to increase diversity in the creative industries through internships, apprenticeships, and other entry routes for young people from under-represented backgrounds.

This brings us to an even more damaging element of gender inequality because, when it comes to representation in the media, the fight for gender equality often crosses over into, and sometimes clashes with, the fight for racial equality, and black women are at the epicentre of these two struggles. They have a fight on two fronts:

they must negotiate a society that discriminates against them because of their gender, and also imposes upon them a standard of female beauty that is at the other end of the spectrum to what they represent. And all in a patriarchal society where women are judged primarily by their appearance before they even say or do anything.

It is in this context that we find the labels of the 'strong black woman' who overcomes opposition and adversity, and the 'angry black woman' who is loud and unreasonable. In the UK and US, women who are given these labels soon become aware that they were not meant to be the delicate damsel rescued by the hero we see depicted in Disney movies. In fact, in order to be worthy of acceptance they need to become as close as they can manage to their white counterparts by suppressing the essence of their authenticity, i.e. their 'blackness'. The burden of women being judged by their appearance before all else is, therefore, especially damaging for women of colour.

So it is that black women in corporate front-of-house roles are often told that their natural Afro hair or braided styles are unacceptable, and that chemical treatments or weaves and wigs that give the appearance of straighter hair are preferable. Even then, wigs and weaves can become a means of denigration, as black US congresswoman Maxine Waters found when US political commentator Bill O'Reilly of Fox News claimed he 'couldn't hear what she was saying because of her James Brown wig!'

As a black woman in the media, I have my own wounds and scars from some of the prejudice, rejection, and subtle slights I have faced throughout my career. I learned very early on that the rules were not the same for me, and that my point of difference, although an asset in most cases, was also sometimes a liability.

One incident that comes to mind was when I was around 21. I had not long been at MTV, yet had one of the highest-rated shows on the network: *MTV Dancefloor Chart*. I was succeeded by Russell Brand when I went to co-present *MTV Select* with British comedian Richard Blackwood. It was a great time in the channel's history – I was part of a wave of MTV VJs (video jockeys) that included Cat Deeley, Edith Bowman, Donna Air, and Sara Cox. We were young, hip, and the voice of Generation X. MTV had just newly rebranded in the UK and Ireland, and the network comms team embarked on an extensive marketing campaign to promote the faces of the channel. This involved a *Sky Magazine* cover titled 'MmmmTV . . . Delicious Reasons to Watch MTV'. The cover was a substantial beauty spread that included every female MTV presenter, except me – even though, at the time, my show was riding high in the ratings and I was a firm favourite with the viewers. My heart sank as I walked past newsstands and saw the cover glaring at me. I was happy for my colleagues but couldn't help crying at the fact that I'd been excluded.

What happened next completely raised my spirits though. Because it was such a big cover story, the viewers of MTV started calling the network to ask if I had left the channel. The news soon spread that I hadn't left, I just hadn't been included in the shoot. It would later transpire that it wasn't *Sky Magazine* that had vetoed me – rather, it was the MTV PR team, who didn't think I was right for the feature so hadn't put my name forward. I have always been a glass–half-full type of person, and always look for the silver lining where possible. This rejection, painful as it was, ended up working in my favour – more and more viewers kept calling the MTV switchboard to complain. As a result, the MTV press office devised a marketing campaign specifically for me and I ended up shooting a piece for *Sky Magazine* with the legendary David Bailey.

Incidents such as these would continue throughout my career. Many times I would agree to a cover shoot, only to be bumped off at the last minute – something fuelled by the general unspoken belief in the industry that women of colour do not sell magazines, which as demonstrated by *Vogue*'s bestselling 'Black' issue, clearly isn't the case. **So, it's fair to say that women of colour have a double dose of discrimination: we are often ignored and excluded or, worse still, insulted in the media – and sometimes that insult is at the hand of our colleagues.**

Such was the case for stalwart Labour MP Diane Abbott, following the Article 50 vote that awarded Conservative Prime Minister Theresa May the authority to begin the process of leaving the European Union. The Brexit Minister David Davis allegedly attempted to hug Abbott for voting with the government, but apparently her response to his show of affection was a strong verbal rejection. Davis then proceeded to inform a 'friend' about this exchange via text, remarking that he would have to be blind to hug Diane Abbott. Fortunately, this 'friend' leaked Davis's text to the press. As hurtful as this was for Abbott, it was important that Davis's disgraceful disrespect was exposed for all to see.

No doubt critics on the other side of this argument will claim that this was merely a joke, and that chastising David Davis is just another case of political correctness. Well, in this and many other cases, politics needs correcting, as too many women, especially those of us who are black, have been expected to tolerate 'jokes' that men would not want directed at their wives, daughters, or sisters. This very public example of misogyny in the workplace helped shine a spotlight on the ways in which black women are stereotyped and denigrated on a daily basis.

This treatment can prompt a heightened sensitivity, especially when your experiences have taught you that this type of unfair abuse can come from anywhere at any time. With no expectation of being defended by wider society, many of us are left with no choice but to defend ourselves, sometimes robustly, hence the term 'angry black woman', which is propagated in the media and society generally. This can be the case even when we have broken barriers and succeeded against all odds, whether it be Michelle Obama being branded an 'ape',[8] or Venus Williams being called a 'gorilla',[9] or Viola Davis deemed 'less classically beautiful' by the *New York Times*.[10]

Michelle Obama eloquently discussed this issue with Oprah Winfrey in her final TV interview before leaving the White House. When she addressed how she dealt with being labelled an 'angry black woman' in her early days as First Lady, and how she rose above this to change the hearts and minds of America and show the world who she really was, she told Oprah, 'I don't hold on to the bad stuff. As black women, there's so much that comes at us all the time, every day, in subtle ways that could tear your soul apart if you let it. But my mother always taught me, "Girl, you better keep it moving." You know, you have to brush it off.'[11]

She is completely right that one has to adopt an extra layer of resilience in order to deal with this kind of discrimination. The one benefit of not receiving adequate or equal validation from the outside world is that it means you go inside yourself to draw upon your own self-esteem, and, in the end, that is the only thing you can truly rely on anyway. This applies to *all* women. When we learn to feel good about ourselves in spite of what the outside world might say, eventually that level of authentic confidence, whatever your gender or hue, is undeniable and the outside world eventually follows suit. It's infectious – we all know it when we see it and can't help but want to be around it. In the end self-love and self-acceptance trump sexism and racism.

But that fact cannot absolve the media of its responsibility. It is imperative that industry bosses change their thinking and ensure that everyone is in the room when the decisions are made, and that they are reflecting and including their audience – *all* of their audience. At the very least this is good business sense, as women will consume the stories that they can see themselves in, but it's also sound moral sense. Harbouring unrealistic ideals of women or a lack of interest in their lives denigrates men as well as women, and can only lead to dissatisfaction, on both sides, with the real thing.

Power in the Workplace

The gender confidence gap is real. **70 per cent of girls believe that they are not 'good enough' in some way** (including in looks, education, and/or relationships).[1] This is understandable: for centuries, women have been told that they are not good enough to receive an education; not good enough to be able to vote; not good enough to have the same jobs, power, and pay as men. They have been told this so often that deep down they have learned to believe it, even though their conscious mind knows it isn't true. So, sometimes, we women are our own worst barrier to change due to our learned self-criticism – our internalized misogyny, which cements our status as not good enough, not quite at home with success.

As things stand, **just 4 per cent of CEO positions in Fortune 500 companies are held by women. None of these positions are held by a black woman. That's 0 per cent.** In fact, **if you're a FTSE 100**

CEO, you're more likely to be called 'John' than to be a woman.[2]

This is bad for business. FACT. It's also bad for society – with a distinct lack of female role models in business, how can we expect our daughters to strive to run their own companies, and be their own bosses? We must confront our self-criticism – and allow other women the space to do this – if we are to achieve gender equality in business.

So many of us, myself included, suffer from 'Imposter Syndrome', perfectly described by Sheryl Sandberg in her 2013 book, *Lean In*:

> *Many people, but especially women, feel fraudulent when they are praised for their accomplishments. Instead of feeling worthy of recognition, they feel undeserving and guilty, as if a mistake has been made. Despite being high achievers, even experts in their fields, women can't seem to shake the sense that it is only a matter of time until they are found out for who they really are – impostors with limited skills or abilities.*[3]

I spend hours on the phone with one of my best friends dissecting the multiple layers of this syndrome, which can manifest in a range of ways – from simple self-deprecation to all-out self-sabotage.

We decided the best way to tackle our Imposter Syndrome was to name and shame it, sort of like Beyoncé/Sasha Fierce in reverse. The only name suitable for such a destructive foe? *Agyness* (no offence to any Agynesses out there). And the funny thing with Agyness is that she is unpredictable; you have no idea when she is going to rear her pernicious head. And, when she does, she can wreak havoc.

A while back, Agyness had tricked me into believing she was finally gone for good. I had been overdosing on 'you can do it' books and thought I was permanently rid of her. While riding this Agyness-free wave, I was invited by Bill Clinton's team to present at his annual Clinton Global Initiative (CGI) opening gala. The line-up included Matt Damon, Eva Longoria, Angélique Kidjo, Carlos Slim, and many more luminaries from the worlds of business, public life, entertainment, and philanthropy. I was brimming with excitement, and felt a million dollars as I waltzed onto the stage in a black-beaded evening gown to introduce Seal, who was performing that evening. Perhaps, I thought, I was finally worthy enough to rendezvous in these revered circles ... Wrong!

The next day, during the CGI preliminary session, Agyness returned with a bang. President Obama was delivering a speech on women and gender equality, so the room was packed full. Even so, somehow among the 600 or so people, I managed to sit next to Jochen

Zeitz, former CEO of Sport & Lifestyle for the Kering Group (owners of luxury fashion brands such as Gucci, Puma, and Alexander McQueen). Jochen has been a real pioneer in ethical fashion and is the co-founder, with Sir Richard Branson, of The B-Team – an organization that is committed to business fairness. Needless to say, I'm a huge fan of his work. For months I'd been trying to secure him as a speaker at a conference I was organizing and was having difficulty finding the best route to reach him – and here it had been handed to me on a plate.

As I opened my mouth to introduce myself, Agyness took over and I froze. I couldn't speak, my palms began to sweat, and I was overcome with insecurity and self-doubt. Agyness was on a roll, bombarding me with numerous reasons as to why I shouldn't ask him to speak at our next event. An hour passed, he even smiled a few times, but I averted my eyes and looked to the floor. Eventually, he and his team left.

That was a pivotal moment for me; a moment when I let fear win the day. What was different this time, compared to when I was walking onto that stage? Why did I make a choice to play it safe rather than risk rejection? On another occasion, there could have been an entirely different outcome; there have been plenty of times in my life when opportunities have presented themselves and I've jumped at them, because in that particular moment I was feeling confident and sure of my abilities. I've nicknamed this event a 'Jochen Moment' – basically the opposite of a light-bulb moment. Fortunately, 'Jochen Moments' do not occur as much as they used to, but when they do, Agyness is usually lurking somewhere not too far away.

This story has a happy ending: a few years later I did manage to summon up the courage to ask and, yes, Jochen did end up speaking at one of my events. I had a second chance. I got lucky. But so often in life, and especially in business, there are no second chances. Courage requires risking failure and rejection, an acceptance of being other than perfect – something we don't allow women to prepare for.

My cousin Reg has an interesting theory about this. He believes that part of the reason men are better at dealing with rejection is because of the practice they get in the dating arena. According to Reg, from the time boys hit puberty and start asking people out, 'no' is a word they become well acquainted with. Therefore, they take 'no' less personally, and see it as a numbers game. As far as Reg is concerned, for every ten women he asks out at least one is bound to say yes – two if he's lucky. Those aren't bad odds.

And he might actually have a point. The **research suggests that in the workplace men *are* better at**

dealing with rejection than women, and certainly don't judge themselves as harshly. Sharon Vosmek, founder and CEO of Astia (a US not-for-profit organization that supports women-led businesses), cites a study by Professor Shelley Correll at the Clayman Institute for Gender Research at Stanford University, which monitored the reactions of 'C' grade calculus degree students. This is what Vosmek described:

> *The men were perceiving they had passed and were wizards, and would potentially use it to go on and negotiate a higher salary. Women in the same calculus class – the majority would drop the course, perceiving they had failed and never mention it again.*[4]

It turns out that Agyness, and my 'Jochen Moment', are classic female responses, hardwired from centuries of gender conditioning. It forced me to face my insecurities and stop avoiding the fact that they existed, something I had been doing my whole adult life.

Using Reg's theory as my guide for healing, I decided to develop an 'Agyness Challenge' based on Jason Comely's 'Rejection Therapy'. Comely, a Canadian entrepreneur, devised a social self-help 'game' for overcoming a fear of rejection, whereby to 'win' required you to receive at least one rejection each day for a period of time, with the intention of training yourself to overcome the fear through extended exposure.

Do this today:

1. Be more aware of how irrational social fears control and restrict our lives.
2. Smash the tyranny of fear and reap the treasures (treasures include wealth, relationships, and self-confidence).
3. Learn from, and even enjoy, rejection.
4. Do not be attached to outcomes, especially when it involves the free agency of other people.
5. Permit yourself to fail.

What's worked for me? A few things. I've journaled which of my career choices have been led by Agyness, and which by my confident self. I also do simple things, like seeking advice or mentorship from people I admire – this can be by cold email, or by approaching them at events and seminars. I force myself to do this much more than I am naturally comfortable with. Even though I work in television and on the surface seem to be very much an extrovert, I am actually quite shy, so this is a real effort for me. However, the benefits far outweigh the safety of staying in my comfort zone.

I urge women everywhere to challenge their own Agyness. We have to learn not to take rejection personally, and rather view it as part of the pathway to success. Once women allow themselves to fear that they are not pretty enough, not clever enough, not strong enough, they behave in a way that limits themselves and makes their dreams less likely to come to fruition. I don't know if it's ever possible to rid ourselves 100 per cent of our Agyness – a lifetime of conditioning cannot be erased overnight. However, facing rejection head-on means you become desensitized to it and better equipped to rise above it, which will help level the playing field not just for ourselves but for future generations.

It's not just women who will benefit. The influence that working women can have on the fortunes of a nation cannot be overstated – and the presence or absence of a strong female workforce has a far wider-reaching effect than most people realize.

It was Mao Zedong who originally said: 'Women hold up half the sky' – and communist China is an interesting case study to draw on when it comes to proving the power of women at work. A few years ago, I was filming in China and interviewed a 90-year-old Wey Chinese woman. The Wey are China's Muslim community and, traditionally, they have been somewhat discriminated against by wider Chinese society. This woman was alive pre-communism, and recounted to me how she felt that, as a woman, she'd had more opportunity under communism than she'd had before. This was in part due to the 1950 Land Reform Act.

Being a proud and firm believer in democracy, I was surprised to hear this – and keen to hear more of her story. So I learnt how the Land Reform Act was devised to improve the economic conditions of peasant workers through land redistribution – and how, as a result, women were allowed to own property, and had equal rights to work the land, marking a huge shift in the traditional role of women in rural Chinese society.

There was more. During China's 'Great Leap Forward' (1958–1960), the government's industrial push demanded that large numbers of men and women work in the newly formed state-owned industries. During this time, the Chinese government also supported women to establish Small and Medium Enterprises (SMEs) in their local communities. These female-owned enterprises and new government initiatives provided jobs for over 180,000 women in Beijing alone.

Long-term, of course, this freedom to work didn't make things better for women. A few decades of policies that advanced women could not alter centuries of Chinese preference for boys. And, as the Chinese population grew exponentially, the government was forced to implement a one-child-per-family policy, which resulted in mass illegal sex-selective abortions and the abandonment of millions of baby girls. Those of age during the 1980s and 1990s will remember seeing the startling images of Chinese baby girls left by the roadside to die, or the numbers of unwanted Chinese girls discarded in orphanages for Westerners to adopt.

However, when it comes to GDP, China is still reaping the rewards of its earlier female-friendly policies. By including women in the workplace and encouraging entrepreneurship amongst its female population the economy was able to grow exponentially, and **China is expected to overtake the USA as the world's largest economy in around 2027**, with some economists predicting that this could happen as soon as 2020. A big obstacle, though, are the unforeseen side-effects of the one-child policy and the gender imbalance it has caused.

A preference for baby boys over girls means that, long-term, China's dominance is precarious. It is estimated that there are 120 boys for every 100 girls – far above the global average and leaving this vast country with 50 million fewer women than men. This has left the economy short of millions of workers. Citigroup economists warn that this in turn could cut 3 per cent off China's GDP.[5] China is going to have to develop emergency measures to tackle the potential economic and social havoc that could be created from its female shortfall. Traditionally, China has not been pro-immigration, but soon it may have no choice – there will be jobs that need filling and men who need marrying.

What can we learn from China? When you create an environment that favours one group, you of course get inequality and under-representation of other groups within elite sectors. This means that you miss the chance to witness the might of human potential and what is possible for all groups if everyone is afforded the same opportunities and supportive treatment. Some gatekeepers – the influencers and decision makers – may still believe in the innate superiority or suitability of one group over others. But the irony here is that unless you, as a gatekeeper, are prepared to be proved wrong, you will never know for sure.

One country that has certainly proved this theory is Rwanda. It has one of the largest female workforces in the world and, as a result, now has one of the fastest-growing economies. Sadly, this shift towards women in the workplace came as an unintended consequence of a horrific civil war. The rise of women in

Rwanda was out of necessity rather than design, after the 1994 genocide wiped out a considerable slice of the working-age male population – many of whom were the senior leaders and officials. A report by the Harvard Kennedy School Review states: 'Prior to 1994, women only held between 10 and 15 per cent of seats in Parliament. Out of sheer necessity, and a desire to rebuild their country, women stepped up as leaders in every realm of the nation, including politics.'[6]

Therefore, Rwanda had no choice but to develop and promote its women into the highest levels of commerce and power. But the benefits have been huge – not only economically, but also socially and politically. Rwanda is the only nation in the world to meet the UN MDGs (Millennium Development Goals), and its Parliament is now 64 per cent female. My view is that this is a shift too far – male dominance should not be replaced with female dominance, but rather with gender parity. But it's a huge step in the right direction. There is much to be learned from the economic promotion of women in Rwanda and China, but our mature democracies mean that we in the West can lead the way in creating a truly gender-equal society.

Nicholas Kristof and Sheryl WuDunn also come to the conclusion that the economic benefits of female empowerment are incontrovertible in their book, *Half the Sky: Turning Oppression into Opportunity for Women*

Worldwide: 'It's no accident that the countries that have enjoyed an economic take-off have been those that educated girls and then gave them the autonomy to move to the cities to find work.'

The evidence suggests that gender equality breeds success at business level, too. A recent report from The Pipeline, a consultancy which aims to help businesses improve diversity at senior levels, shows that '**Profit margins are almost double in companies with at least 25 per cent females on their executive committee, compared to those with only men.**'[7] And women help other women: **female CEOs have on average twice as many women on their executive committees than their male counterparts**[8] – which will, as we've seen, in turn help the bottom line.

These stats speak for themselves: the numbers of women reaching these powerful positions are low, but when they do, they are of huge economic benefit to the company. Despite all our progress, the statistics are still depressingly low. But given the financial rewards that would be reaped, it's clear that the future of business must involve the full and equal inclusion of *all* women.

Of course, it's not as simple as having women in the room. Organisations must pay their women fairly – both from a moral point of view, and, competitively, in order to attract the most talented staff. As has been front-page news this year, the disparity in gender pay despite legislation and much debate remains an unresolved issue.

The BBC found itself as the national symbol of this debate when the alarming pay disparity between its male and female top earners was released last year. The figures revealed that its highest male earner, Chris Evans (annual salary between £2.2m and £2.25m in 2016/2017), earned more than four times that of the Corporation's highest female earner, Claudia Winkleman (annual salary between £450,000 and £499,999).[9] The figures were even bleaker in its news department, which had numerous male presenters earning over £100,000 more than their female colleagues for doing exactly the same job. The BBC was heavily criticized once the salaries of its top earners was made public, and the fallout has been immense, with many of its female onscreen talent threatening legal action. Unfortunately, the BBC gender pay gap appears to be a microcosm of the society it serves as it also reflects a class bias where 45 per cent of the highest paid were privately educated – so **they too are recruiting for the highest-paid positions from the pool of 7 per cent of the UK who are privately educated.**[10]

But there is a reckoning happening where gender parity is concerned. Fortunately, it seems that women are now demanding that companies and employers 'Pay Up'. The recent spate of companies reporting their gender pay gap, including HSBC (59 per cent), Channel 4 (28.6 per cent), the *Guardian* (11.3 per cent), and easyJet (53 per cent) to name a few, has shown the true extent of unequal pay at work in the face of presumed gender parity – and women are no longer willing to accept being paid less for the same work.

When you factor race into the gender pay gap, women of colour fare even worse than their white counterparts. In the BBC, there were **just five black or ethnic minority women on the list of the ninety-six stars who earn more than £150,000**[11]. This is an issue that Serena Williams has made it her mission to highlight. Arguably one of the most success-ful athletes in the world, and definitely at the pinnacle of her sport, she's spoken up about gender and racial disparity in pay not just in her own sport but in society in general:

> *The cycles of poverty, discrimination, and sexism are much, much harder to break than the record for Grand Slam titles . . . Women of color [sic] have to work – on average – eight months longer to earn the same as their male counterparts do in one year.*[12]

In a moving personal essay, published by *Fortune* magazine, the 23-time Grand Slam champion writes that '**for every dollar a white man earns, black**

**women make just 63 cents', while white women
earn 80 cents.**

Her concerns are backed up by many studies, both
in the UK and the US, looking at income inequality,
such as one from the Fawcett Society, which high-
lighted that **black women were among some of the
lowest-paid females, with Pakistani and Bangladeshi
women earning the least among all groups.**[13] This
is clearly not where we want to be as a society. But
we sleepwalk into the situation by disregarding 'others'
even when they are successful (like Serena), and then
wonder why we have endemic issues with pay disparity.
**Fundamentally, we cannot harness the power of
women until we pay them what they are worth.**

In short, if we empower women, we all get richer which
makes winning the argument a no-brainer – because
if we all win, nobody loses, right? Well, that's only if
we forget about intersectionality and all the other forms
of discrimination that women can face by the virtue
of being other than white, heterosexual, able-bodied,
upper/middle class, or being born in a Western Country.
We can't justifiably announce the fight for equality as
won when we know that opportunities for women
differ wildly based on circumstances that are just as
arbitrary as gender. When women unite across these
boundaries and find common purpose without ignoring

the specific challenges that 'other' women face, they are able to bring together the rich diversity of talent to address inequality in all its guises. The fight for gender parity must be inclusive and intersectional.

This is something Gloria Steinem and Dorothy Pitman Hughes understood when they co-founded *Ms* magazine together during the seventies feminist movement. This was decades before the term 'intersectionality' had even been coined, but they lived it – and, as a result, succeeded, because they understood its value. Gloria Steinem credited African-American women with getting feminism started in the US: 'I thought they invented the feminist movement. I know we all have different experiences, but I learned feminism disproportionately from black women.' Working together, Steinem and Pitman Hughes were able to reach wider audiences and were incredibly successful in advancing the cause of second-wave feminism.

As a feminist you cannot and must not only fight for women from your own socio-economic or cultural background. There is a hierarchy of inclusion in society and it's imperative we are all aware of where we are on the ladder and do our utmost to give a hand-up to those who are a few steps lower down – not from a position of pity or superiority but rather from a place of solidarity and sisterhood.

So, if you're an upper-class white woman, ask yourself: are you being inclusive of working class women? If you're an able-bodied heterosexual woman of colour: are you being mindful of disabled or trans women?

Someone who understands the societal and economic benefits of investing in and adequately compensating women is Swiss industrialist Yann Borgstedt. Borgstedt spent the first part of his career building his own business and after a successful exit he 'wanted to share his good fortune and make a positive impact on society', so he used part of the proceeds to create The Womanity Foundation. Womanity is dedicated to empowering disadvantaged women and girls all over the world. Founded in 2005, the Foundation has gone on to change the lives of thousands of women and girls globally in areas including Brazil, the Middle East, Africa, India, and Afghanistan. Listed among the UN's top 500 NGOs, the foundation focuses on girls' education and **helping to end violence against women, which is one of the top preventable causes of death for women globally and 'one of the biggest economic costs to society – £30 billion per year in the UK alone,'** Borgstedt explained when I interviewed him.

Borgstedt is now dedicated to helping close the gender equality gap: 'As a man I could not sit by and let others get the short end of the stick because they were born a woman.' Like many thought leaders and change agents, Borgstedt obviously has a TED Talk, and his is titled 'Why Men Should Invest in Women', which was filmed in London at a TEDx event. Opening boldly, Borgstedt states that his mission is to help 'create a society where men and women are given the same rights and chances'. He passionately reels off stat after stat: '**65 countries lose \$95 billion in GDP by investing less in girls' education than boys; 70 per cent of the world's poor are women; only 1 per cent of property ownership is in the hands of women**'. As he continues he then jokes: 'I'm going to bore you with statistics, but I know if I need to change men's minds then I need to bore them with statistics.'[14]

One thing that is certain is that when it comes to gender equality, the numbers don't lie – both in terms of the severe levels of inequality, the sheer costs financially, and the immense gains, economically and socially, when we get it right. So why are some people so afraid of this? What is the threat inherent in gender equality? Men do not lose from female emancipation. We all win. The payoff, for ourselves and for society, when women push beyond our worthiness barriers is priceless.

Through my work I've been fortunate enough to come up close and personal with some of the most inspirational women of our time – women who fearlessly embody the Sheryl Sandberg philosophy of 'leaning in'; women who defy (present-day) expectations and limitations. These women are creating a *new normal* – one that is centred around female-friendly working practices – and it's being led by women like Mary Callahan Erdoes.

As CEO of J.P. Morgan Asset Management, Callahan Erdoes is one of the most important people in finance and supervises over $2.2 trillion in assets. A wife and mother to three children, she explained to me how she used her seniority to make it easier for other working mothers within her organization. She leaves the office early enough to collect her children from school every day, and loudly announces it daily to her team: 'I'm leaving to go and pick up the kids.'

Another leading working mother who is unapologetic about it is Helena Morrissey, former CEO of Newton Investment Management, a £51 billion Bank of New York Mellon fund. Morrissey is also the co-founder of the 30% Club, a campaign to make UK FTSE 100 boardrooms a minimum of 30 per cent female. She is a trailblazer and has risen to the top of the UK finance industry. However, she is almost as famous for her professional achievements as she is for her nine children, who range in age from nine to twenty-six.

Morrissey leaves the office every day at 6 p.m. to be

home in time for a family dinner. She credits part of her success to having a stay-at-home husband, Richard: 'The idea that a woman can have a family and friends and hold down a difficult, high-octane job when both partners work full-time – that is a very tall order. I am not saying it's impossible, but it's a bit unrealistic.'

Morrissey believes that the key to having it all is for modern couples to determine which career should take precedence while the children are young. And, crucially, this doesn't have to be the man's. In Morrissey's case, after their fourth child was born she and Richard, then a journalist, decided he should stay at home and she should continue with her career – a decision that has paid off considerably. The return on investment (ROI) has not only benefited their family (as Morrissey is one of the highest-paid executives in the city), it's also benefited British society.

Obviously, Callahan Erdoes and Morrissey are unique examples, as these two women are at the very top of their industries. Parent-friendly working practices are easier to implement when you are the boss. However, if more women rise through the corporate ranks, these sorts of flexible working patterns will become more and more commonplace – because they will have to.

We cannot rely on these trailblazing women alone,

though – which is why the new legislation on gender pay transparency is so important. As a society, we need to look again at who we value and how we value them. What methodology are we using for the remuneration of women and men? Business models are often founded on bonus packages, appraisal processes, and promotions based on subjective data that may have a gender bias or be straight-out discriminatory towards women who have family commitments (such as tacit rewards for out-of-hours working). Now that companies and organisations are having to be transparent about their pay gaps we can see the extent of this issue which can no longer be ignored. Clearly it is time to admit that the equal pay legislation is unfortunately not fit for purpose and the government needs to step in with better, more enforceable regulations.

The gender pay gap is both a challenge and potentially an opportunity for Theresa May and her government. Brexit is of course the poisoned chalice of British politics which casts a shadow over Theresa May's premiership and brought her predecessor's reign to an abrupt end. However, despite the referendum result, it was David Cameron's stance and success in delivering marriage equality that has saved his legacy from being defined solely by Brexit. A truly enforceable Equal Pay Act could be the saving grace of Theresa May's legacy and as our second female Prime Minister it seems fitting that she be the person to get this right.

Another stumbling block when it comes to harnessing women's power in the workplace is the lack of role models. Role models are important, for women and men; as Marian Wright Edelman said: *'You can't be what you can't see'*.

I remember having a conversation about this with my friend Toby Daniels, founder of the highly successful Social Media Week conferences. Toby made a point that stopped me in my tracks: 'Men don't see women as role models.' In an attempt to halt my jaw from hitting the floor, he went on to explain:

> *Mark Zuckerberg grew up wanting to be Bill Gates, Jack Dorsey grew up wanting to be Steve Jobs, Marissa Mayer probably looked up to the same male role models as Zuckerberg and Dorsey with a few female ones too. I doubt Zuckerberg and Dorsey would have had female business role models. When we have a woman who creates and is credited for the next ground-breaking innovation that moves humanity forward, such as the next Internet or the next Apple, then there will be a generation of boys and young men wanting to emulate those women.*

I had never even thought about whether or not boys,

or indeed girls, grew up with any female business role models. I've always had a slew of male business icons I've looked up to and whose biographies I've devoured. As it stands, women have many professional male role models, but the reverse is seldom true.

Every female in a leadership position is a role model for a new generation of both men and women about what is possible. One such woman, who's always been one of my favourite role models, is Clare Boothe Luce, a woman who carved out a phenomenal life for herself in mid-twentieth-century America, then very much a man's world. A *Vanity Fair* excerpt from the second volume of Sylvia Jukes Morris's biography of Boothe Luce opens with: 'What Clare Boothe Luce wanted, Clare Boothe Luce got: a man, a seat in Congress, an ambassadorship.' All this was true, but Boothe Luce also managed to achieve so much more. She was able to soar to great heights in three distinctly different careers. Starting out as a journalist, she rose to become managing editor of *Vanity Fair* by 30, making her one of the youngest magazine editors in history. She then tried her hand at playwriting, penning the smash hit *The Women* in 1936, and later the screenplay for the movie *Come to the Stable*, which earned an Oscar nomination in 1949 for Best Writing. After writing came a foray into politics, where she became one of the first women in Congress after running as a

Republican and winning what was then a safe Democratic seat. She rounded out her political career as an ambassador to Italy for the Eisenhower administration.

But all this success came with a pressure, unique to people who represent the minority in their field. Boothe Luce knew that her success or failure would affect not just her personally but the perception of female ability in general. She said:

> *Because I am a woman, I must make unusual efforts to succeed. If I fail, no one will say, "She doesn't have what it takes," they will say, "Women don't have what it takes.*[15] *"*

Any woman who works knows that Boothe Luce's words are as true today as they were when she uttered them over four decades ago. Even so, she never let the barriers she faced prevent her from succeeding. Instead, she used them as motivation to defy expectations for women of her day. But is it really fair to ask that successful women carry this pressure, in addition to the pressures of leading their fields?

Thankfully, both men and women have evolved since Booth Luce's day. The fact that we have come so far so quickly in the last 100 years alone should give us hope but should not encourage us to become complacent. We have a great opportunity to achieve the equality across society that we want, and we have a much better chance of achieving that with men fully involved. Unfortunately, men haven't a great record on achieving equality along class, gender race, or any of the major groupings on their own. We just need to understand that everything from managing a family to managing a country gets better results where men and women work together equally. Also, the gender debate is widening and we need to acknowledge this and be able to reach across gender boundaries to other genders facing their struggles, which are not separate to the fight for gender equality. We must be mindful of a hierarchy of inclusion in society, so to borrow a phrase we've heard from men in battle or warfare, but with a progressive amendment: 'We leave no PERSON behind.' And this, my friends, is why feminism is good for *everyone*!

Power in Numbers

'If you want to go *fast*, go alone. If you want to go *far*, go together.'

African Proverb

Turning to the wider case for gender equality, we must look at one of the abiding hurdles that women frequently come up against: men. I must stress that this is not an opportunity for male-bashing. On the contrary, we must ensure that men are our partners in this process, not our antagonists.

Up until now employment (and financial success) has been the main source and definition whereby men have obtained their self-esteem and position in society, and we must ensure that women sharing that work-space are deemed collaborators rather than a threat. Women can be guilty of using power and wealth to determine what we deem as 'eligible' or 'a catch' – certainly history had this as a worthwhile consideration.

A 2017 report by the Institute of Fiscal Studies (IFS) found that poor men in their forties were twice as likely to be single as men from richer backgrounds.[1] So-called unsuccessful men are made to feel less of a man and less desirable. So, when you weigh it up, on the surface it might look as if men stand to lose a lot more from equality than women – and we haven't yet figured out what the emotional or egoic pay-off will be for them.

Since women look to be the immediate beneficiaries of gender equality (even if we know that in the bigger picture society as a whole benefits), we need to help shape a new narrative for these men and how we are going to relate to them. Things are going to change for both genders, and how we value men in society has to change to reflect this. Our idea of success needs to be redefined; women have the opportunity to lead the way on this and show our male counterparts that they need not fear a successful woman.

As the world changes, modern men are facing a challenge to their roles at home and in the world at large. Political changes have given women the right to challenge male dominance and to compete with men in what was once considered their domain. For boys in the playground who have always been socialized to be competitive go-getters (after all, that's what you need to be in a capitalist economy), there is no greater shame than 'losing to a girl'. Men are used to competing with other men but don't know what a 'fair fight' with a woman looks like. Do they keep them at arm's length, or try to recreate an environment of traditional male supremacy and hope that the woman reverts to type? Neither of these approaches works.

Socially and culturally, we have moved far away from the traditional definition of the male. Men now share their gender space with those who don't have old-fashioned male attributes and may well be more successful than 'traditional' men. Creative men, so-called 'effeminate men', transgender men, gay men, designers, artists, chefs, performers, and models have all challenged the traditional view of what a man should be, which for some has created a crisis of identity and image. What should the twenty-first-century man be able to do? What should he be able to acquire? What should he look like? Who should he love? How should he love?

The man in the house is no longer the man *of* the house in the traditional sense. He may not be solely responsible for providing financial security, the home may not be in his name, and the children in it may not be biologically his. Being a father was always about providing for your children, not so much about how you interacted with them, and being a husband was about protecting your wife rather than supporting her.

But with those certainties no longer certain, what then is the man's role in that house? At this point I can't but emphasize the value not just of empowering women, but of collaboration between the sexes.

The Obamas are a particularly strong example of a couple who have redefined what a truly equal partnership looks like. Barack Obama is one of the few men in the public eye over the past decade to have presented a response to the question of the new male identity for the twenty-first century. Yes, politically he was the first African-American president, but almost as radical was his portrayal or interpretation of what it means to be a modern man. A man who had not served in the military, as many previous presidents had, but who positioned himself to be judged not only on his performance in his job but as a husband and a father too, indicating that his ability in those areas was an equally important measure of a man. As president, he would routinely reference the impact of his decisions as a father of two daughters, and gave a clear message that his wife Michelle was his equal and partner in his role as POTUS, and that it was his role to support and honour her as FLOTUS as much as it was hers to support him.

Michelle in turn often had her own platform and spoke out on many issues, which complemented and enhanced her husband as a president and a man. It was obvious that she had been his constant collaborator in his unlikely journey to the White House. Clearly as a man he had been discerning in his choice of partner and not been afraid of intelligence, ambition, and strong opinions when he encountered them. He did not view these as a threat to his masculinity, but rather as an enhancement. As a couple, and a true and equal union, the Obamas present a redefined view of masculinity and femininity within the context of traditional marriage, and are a living embodiment of Margaret Mead's powerful quote: 'Every time we *liberate a woman, we liberate a man.*'

And of course, as a result, the Obama brand is huge. **Barack Obama has 17 million followers on Instagram; Michelle Obama has 20 million.** Obama's posts about or featuring Michelle Obama invariably get several times as many likes than his others (for instance, a post on climate change and the Paris Agreement received 415k likes, whereas a photo of him and Michelle captioned 'Happy Valentine's Day @michelleobama. You make every day and every place better' received 3.5 million. How many of his 17 million followers would be following him without the Michelle factor? And yet even those who were first attracted to his feed for snaps of his marriage will hear and be influenced by his political agenda, too.

Real wonders can be achieved when men and women work together, utilizing each other's strengths and even compensating where the other may be lacking. Great dynasties, empires, and companies have been built, maintained, and expanded through such collaborations. Any entity or venture that interacts with people to persuade them to act in a particular way will be dealing with both men and women, so to have an understanding and empathy of both is essential to success. This might seem obvious, but in many cases the greatest collaborations have been obscured from our view as the female in the partnership has played a hidden role, which suits our preconceived ideas of a male/female partnership.

I believe this is in part why society is so obsessed with 'power couples' – high-profile couples where a man and a woman become more than the sum of their parts. They are 'all good' by themselves, but a force when they're together. There are many examples in today's media – JAY-Z and Beyoncé; the Beckhams. In the UK we now have our own new Royal 'Power Couple' in the union of Prince Harry and Meghan Markle – the new Duke and Duchess of Sussex. Markle was a career woman in her own right and a self-proclaimed feminist before meeting Prince Harry. Her brand of modern feminism has brought a new wave of support for the Royal family, and the pair have already spoken about the positive impact they wish to make on the world. However, let's not forget this is not the first dynamic royal couple. We can also go back over a century to one of the most effective power couples of all time: Queen Victoria and Prince Albert. Theirs was a unique relationship in an era when men were shaping the world and women still couldn't vote: a queen who ruled over an empire, and her husband, who was her consort but also her subject. This, as you might imagine, must have been a very delicate situation for Albert's male ego. But, rather than compete with one another, Victoria and Albert celebrated each other's strengths, and together this formidable pair were great patrons of science and the arts, and their shared vision helped to ignite a century of innovation while also securing the future of the British monarchy.

It's clear that where men and women complement and balance each other, partnerships flourish and great things can happen. This is not only the case in the romantic arena; the same is true in business. One such example is the professional partnership of Angela Ahrendts and Christopher Bailey. During their successful reign at Burberry, this dynamic duo turned a failing British heritage label into one of the most successful and innovative fashion brands in the world.

We all have men in our lives over whom we have some influence. And we all need to hold these men accountable by encouraging and celebrating their progressive practices at work and at home, thus enabling our husbands, partners, brothers, and sons to see the advantages to a workplace of ambitious and effective female colleagues. It is by collaborating with the men in our own lives, holding them to account when we need to, that we'll see the shift we need on the global stage.

Because the real crux of the problem is, without a doubt, how men and women relate to each other in general: how we are socialized and schooled as children, and how this impacts the way we interact as adults. If we drill down a little further, most leadership positions are still the domain of an elite group of privileged men. Many of these men have been educated in the private system, which tends to separate boys and girls. If you haven't grown up collaborating with girls on your end-of-year science project, then you're less likely to feel comfortable collaborating with women in your adult life.

As a state-school-educated woman of colour, I have been negatively impacted by these institutionalized standards that benefit white men from privileged back-grounds. But I've benefited, too – we all have. We can't deny that some of the world's most innovative inventions have been created by this small, elite group and their equivalents from the rest of Europe, the US, and beyond. For example, many of us today are able to enjoy travelling by land, sea, and air thanks to the endeavours of Henry Ford, John Fitch, and the Wright brothers.

However, there is a plethora of unsung female inventors who have helped to move society forward, too – and there would undoubtedly be even more if women had historically had the same access to education and opportunity as men. I'm thinking of women such as Maria Beasley, who saved millions of lives with her invention of the life raft in 1882, and Mary Walton, who created several key air and noise pollutionreducing devices and mechanisms, also in the late nineteenth century. Or Stephanie Kwolek, one of the first female research chemists, credited in 1971 with the invention of Kevlar®, a synthetic material five times as strong as steel that is the main ingredient in bulletproof vests. Or 12-year-old Rachel Zimmerman, who, in the 1980s, developed a software program using 'Blissymbols', which enabled people who have difficulty speaking – such as those with severe physical disabilities like cerebral palsy – to communicate.

Then you have women such as Katherine Johnson, Dorothy Vaughan and Mary Jackson, three African-American NASA mathematicians whose unsung genius was vital in getting the US into the space exploration game. Their ground-breaking story was depicted in the 2016 movie *Hidden Figures*, which to date has grossed over $224 million worldwide at the box office[2] and inspired a generation of young girls to study STEM (Science, Technology, Engineering, and Maths).

And yet, just **48 women have been awarded a Nobel Prize between 1901 and 2017 – compared to 844 men.**[3]

In Britain, one of our own 'hidden figures' marks perhaps one of the greatest injustices in scientific history. When it comes to the discovery of DNA, many people have heard of James Watson, Francis Crick, and Maurice Wilkins – the three male scientists who shared the Nobel Prize for this momentous scientific breakthrough – but few have heard of Rosalind Franklin, the woman whose work in the area of crystallography and X-ray diffraction provided the image of the famed 'Photo 51' that Watson and Crick used as the basis for their now-iconic model of DNA. Franklin had innocently given Wilkins, her colleague at King's College, access to the image, not knowing that he would later reveal it to her Cambridge rivals, Watson and Crick. When they published their findings in the scientific *Nature* magazine in April 1953, they downplayed their use of Franklin's research. Sadly, Franklin died from ovarian cancer in 1958. She was only 37 and her vital contribution to the discovery of DNA was never fully recognized in her lifetime. Fortunately, her brilliance was not overlooked permanently and history has been kind to her legacy – she is now regarded as one of the most important scientists of the twentieth century.[4]

These women were exceptional, not because their gender lacked ability, but because they managed to thrive in industries where progression might be restricted or prohibited due to their gender. Imagine how much faster and more innovatively we could progress without those barriers in place! By high-lighting the scientific achievements of women like Rosalind Franklin, we can encourage more young girls to develop a passion for STEM and to believe that women have a vital role to play in the area of science and technology.

If all gatekeepers – the educators, the decision makers, the employers, and the influencers – had the same visionary approach that enabled women like Katherine Johnson, Dorothy Vaughan, and Mary Jackson to progress, imagine how much richer our world would be. Unfortunately, not all gatekeepers do, which begs the question: what has been the cost to us all? Or, to put it another way, how much longer will we have to wait for a cure for AIDS, a solution to our environmental issues, or a resolution to today's geopolitical and socioeconomic concerns, if men and women fail to work together and allow mutual progression? That is the real cost of holding back or denying potential brilliance, because it comes in unexpected packaging.

The Power of Persuasion

It's clear that, socially and culturally, we are limited by a shocking lack of gender equality on the global stage. By working together, we can change this. To do my bit to address the issue, in 2010, with the support of Sarah Brown, Arianna Huffington, and Donna Karan, I co-founded Women: Inspiration and Enterprise (WIE), a women's conference in New York City with Dee Poku.[1] How WIE came about was really a case of being in the right place at the right time. I had not long moved to America when, in November 2009, Sarah Brown (wife of then UK PM Gordon Brown) invited me to a women's empowerment dinner she was hosting in New York with Queen Rania, Indra Nooyi (CEO of Pepsico), and Wendi Deng Murdoch. Really, the evening was the Oscars of women's empowerment – and one of the most A-list rooms I have ever seen in my life. Guests in attendance included everyone from Nicole Kidman to Ivanka Trump (prior to her father becoming President), and from Naomi Campbell to Jessica Alba.

Sarah Brown delivered a heartfelt speech where she urged every woman to commit to doing something to help another woman. I was lucky enough to be sat next to Brigid McConville, the UK CEO of the White Ribbon Alliance (WRA), and – in a momentary Agyness-free second – we stood up and said we were going to organize some sort of event. Afterwards, Sarah Brown walked over to our table to discuss it further, and said she would provide whatever support was needed – and she did.

Because we had made the announcement to this esteemed room (without really knowing what we were letting ourselves in for!), it felt like there was no turning back. Months later, we were organizing a press conference with Sarah, who had roped in her friend Arianna Huffington, plus Donna Karan who had been brought in by a friend of mine. Now there really *was* no turning back.

WIE was conceived with the ethos of women inspiring women and developing a dialogue on how we can all be our best selves. The aim was to create a forum in which this generation's leaders could empower the next generation and then pay it forward to women in the developing world.

The focus of the first two years of WIE was to highlight the phenomenal work of the White Ribbon Alliance, a global charity committed to reducing maternal mortality. Sarah Brown and the WRA (of which Sarah is a global patron) have been instrumental in getting this issue on the global agenda and included as part of the UN Millennium Development Goals. Their ground-breaking work also encouraged Bill and Melinda Gates to start investing heavily in the fight against maternal mortality.

Dee and I had a magnificent time working alongside the senior WRA team, which included Betsy McCallon, Brigid McConville, and Jo Cox. The lead-up to our first NYC WIE conference was some of the most fun I've had in my working life. We were a team of five women, all committed to creating an event that would uplift and inspire, while also raising awareness for a great cause. The atmosphere was collaborative and one of female camaraderie. I was able to experience first-hand what a female-engineered professional environment looks like, as for almost ten months we all worked remotely on the event. I was in LA, Dee was in New York, Betsy was in Washington DC, and Brigid and Jo were in London. We were a team of novices on a very tight budget, so there were many close calls, but we handled and solved them together via our weekly conference calls and flurry of daily emails.

I still remember with fondness the day we were all actually in the same room. It was a hot September evening in New York during UNGA (UN General

Assembly) week. I already knew Brigid and Betsy well, but it was my first time meeting Jo in person, who was heavily pregnant at the time with her first child. She was a bundle of energy, whose fierce intellect, wit, and cheeky grin were simply infectious. She was carrying a boy and we all agreed that this WIE baby would one day become the type of feminist man we were trying to promote with our conference. None of us knew back in 2010 the tragic turn of events that would cut Jo's magnificent life short six years later, but what is certain is that she didn't just talk the talk – she lived it and inspired everyone she encountered to do the same.

Every day we see people like Jo working for change – and one might assume that women are well on their way to overcoming prejudice and achieving equality. Unfortunately, the very idea of equality still faces opposition – from women as well as men. You could argue that race rather than gender was the biggest dividing line in America, but Americans have twice voted in a black president, but they didn't vote in a woman to lead them when they had the chance. Hillary Clinton did, of course, manage to win the popular vote by almost 3 million in the 2016 US election, but she failed to secure the votes from the majority of her own demographic. **Donald Trump received 53 per** cent of the white female vote in the presidential election,[2] and his campaign was anything but female-friendly.

Trump advocated that women be punished for choosing to terminate unwanted pregnancies, and during one of the presidential debates, when asked about a recording in which he bragged about sexually predatory behaviour against women, his response was that the US had a problem with political correctness and his comments were just 'locker-room talk'. Over a dozen women accused him of sexual assault, but even this, it seems, did not deter female voters from choosing him over Hillary Clinton.

There are a multitude of reasons why people vote the way they do, but the fact that the majority of white females voted for a man with a very narrow view of the value of women over a female candidate with much more experience suggests that in America it's not only men who have an issue with a female commander-in-chief. This may be the most powerful example we've yet seen of internalized misogyny. America may be the leader of the free world, but in terms of female leadership it still has a long way to go.

In 2018, the UK is on its second female prime minister and has had a female head of state for the last six decades, but there is no cause for congratulations or complacency in gender parity here either. We don't yet have a level gender playing field anywhere in the world.

And yet the argument for parity for women is overwhelming. We've seen the evidence that it is essential for economic growth; for technological advancement; and for stronger, happier, and more powerful relationships between men and women. We've seen that the misrepresentation and exclusion of women in the media feeds unhealthy stereotypes, encourages insecurity in women, and leads to a narrow demographic appeal and a lack of relatable role models for women and for men. We've seen that women can excel in the boardroom as much as men, while still maintaining their role in family life. And we've seen that this parity would in fact benefit men, not detract from them. So, everyone really is a winner.

We have already made great headway on gender equality. In the last fifty years especially, the landscape at home and at work and on the global stage has changed significantly for women. But there is still a lot of work to do if we are to continue making progress and, crucially, if we are to prevent it from rolling backwards. Astrologists say we've now entered the Age of Aquarius – the feminine age when women will step into leadership roles like never before, and a feminine dynamic will begin to balance the scales of power. These are indeed exciting times for women, but to navigate them to our fullest potential, we need to decide how we're going to shape and influence the workplace and power structure in a way that is authentic to who we are as women, rather than stepping into the male template. For decades women have fitted themselves as square pegs into male-designed round holes, but what does success on female terms look like? How will women redefine the attributes society considers successful, and how will we select what those attributes are? To answer these questions in the twenty-first century, gender equality has to be at the forefront of government social policy.

Gender mainstreaming is about making women's issues into men's issues, too. As Emmeline Pankhurst said: 'We have to free half of the human race, the women, so that they can help to free the other half.' This has to be a goal that men and women work together on, so that the outcome brings shared success, rather than resentment or emasculation. This will set the framework for how we create a society in which women are valued just as much as their male counterparts. And, in achieving that, we will all reap the rewards of the talent that will be unleashed.

Afterword
The Power of Role Models

History is written by the winners, and far too often in our history even winning women ultimately have been on the losing side, their brilliance and valuable contribution no match for centuries of an entrenched patriarchy and institutional misogyny.

Even in the face of insurmountable inequality there have been countless female leaders to admire, but unfortunately we have not celebrated them as we should. We do not immortalize them with great statues and monuments or public bank holidays; many great women's contributions have been all but forgotten. In fact, it was only this year we finally saw the first female commemorated in Parliament Square.

As a leader in the women's suffrage movement Millicent Fawcett paved the way for the UK to become a full democracy with women allowed to vote and eventually take up seats in the building outside which her likeness now proudly stands. She is arguably the individual most deserving of a space in Parliament Square, as her actions have had a direct impact on its composition.

The reason I am highlighting this is because I believe it is important for all genders to have female role models as a vital element to seeing women as equals and as potential leaders. Here is an 'easy win' if you want to support gender equality: research and educate yourself about a woman from the past or present that you can admire. Then inform others about her, by referencing her story or achievements in general conversation or as part of your work, particularly if you are a teacher or trainer or someone who has to speak to groups of people. In this way you are educating yourself, as well as both your social and professional circles, about female excellence.

As I'm a woman who likes to practice what she preaches, I would like to share the story of a female heroine of mine who is not so well known in Western society, but is literally a legend and national hero in Ghana, especially amongst the Ashanti people. The Ghanaian culture (especially Ashanti) is essentially matriarchal and therefore people of Ghanaian heritage like myself are raised to see female strength as normal and natural. As a result, the women in my family have always been very opinionated – a trait which I can happily say hasn't bypassed me. Every Ghanaian child is taught about Yaa Asantewaa, our own African Warrior Queen, the woman who took on the might of an empire, like Boudica, and inspired men to fight against a foreign foe when all seemed lost (like the first Queen Elizabeth).

The story of Yaa Asantewaa is set during the European scramble for Africa in the nineteenth century. Britain wanted to expand its Gold Coast colony (present-day Ghana) and subdue the Ashanti Kingdom which threated their authority in the region. Lengthy brutal battles meant the Ashanti Kingdom had taken a bit of a bruising from the British, who had superior weaponry. It seemed all was lost, and the Ashanti king was about to accept defeat risking the fate of the Golden Stool, the ancient royal divine throne which the Ashanti believe houses the spirit of the Ashanti nation. However Yaa, the Queen Mother, had other ideas. The role of the Queen Mother is incredibly significant in Ashanti royal custom; she is an advisor who choses a male member of the female line to inherit the Kingship and is ultimately the moral gatekeeper of the family and tribe. So Yaa had influence which she was about to bring to bear; The Queen

Mother rallied all the Ashanti women to take up arms against the British invaders and prepared to lead them into battle with or without the male warriors. This act of defiance served to shame the male warriors into remembering their duty to fight and defend the sovereignty of the Ashanti nation. However, shaming the men into action wasn't Yaa's only tactic; the Queen Mother also delivered a powerful speech and inspired the men into remembering the brave warriors they were, which empowered them to seize victory over the British imperial forces. Known as the 'War of the Golden Stool', Yaa Asantewaa's leadership in this monumental battle is celebrated and revered as an example that women are as powerful as men, and that true partnership between the sexes can result in significant success or even indeed save a nation.

Eventually, the British conquered the Ashanti, but the integrity of Ashanti as a kingdom and a culture endured even through colonisation and independence up to the present day. This long-lasting cultural pride is in part due to Yaa Asantewaa's bravery and is something the people of Ghana have never forgotten. Her story exemplifies what women can achieve when they are able to express the fullness of their potential: leading, counselling, and inspiring others regardless of gender. So I call on you to choose your Yaa Asantewaa and champion her story wherever you go, so that female role models become as commonplace as male ones. Because, as we know, perception engenders reality. And if we change perception, we *can* change reality.

Notes and References

The Empowered Women

1. 39% of women vs. 37% of men live in poverty in the UK; 15% of women to 12% of men in the USA. From the Women's Budget Group and the Census Bureau respectively.
2. Office for National Statistics
3. *The Power of Parity: Advancing women's equality in the United Kingdom* by Vivian Hunt, et al., McKinsey Global Institute Report, September 2016

Power in the Media

1. *Guardian*: https://www.theguardian.com/media/2013/may/15/female-tv-presenters-ageism-sexism
2. http://womenandhollywood.com/resources/statistics/2017-statistics/
3. https://seejane.org/research-informs-empowers/gender-bias-advertising
4. https://womenandhollywood.com/resources/statistics/

5. http://reelgirl.com/2011/10/stats-from-miss-representation/
6. *Telegraph:* https://www.telegraph.co.uk/films/0/top-3-box-office-hits-2017-had-female-leads-first-time-decades
7. *Standard:* https://www.standard.co.uk/fashion/vanessa-kingori-vogue-edward-enninful-a3827146.html
8. *The Atlantic:* https://www.theatlantic.com/entertainment/archive/2017/11/british-vogue-edward-enninful/545279/
9. BBC: http://www.bbc.co.uk/news/election-us-2016-37985967
10. http://www.news.com.au/sport/tennis/venus-williams-called-gorilla-in-espns-australian-open-commentary/news-story/1b70be84a4fd3c820ecc67ae5f0f7cf9
11. *New York Times:* https://www.nytimes.com/2014/09/21/arts/television/viola-davis-plays-shonda-rhimess-latest-tough-heroine.html?_r=1
12. Oprah Winfrey CBS Special with Michelle Obama, 19 December 2016

Power in the Workplace

1. *Parent 24:* http://www.parent24.com/Teen_13-18/Development/70-of-girls-feel-theyre-not-good-enough-20160629
2. Hampton-Alexander Review: FTSE Women Leaders – Improving gender balance in FTSE leadership: 2017 review, UK Department for Business, Energy & Industrial Strategy, November 2016
3. *Lean In: Women, Work and the Will to Lead* by Sheryl Sandberg (Knopf, 2013)
4. *Telegraph:* http://www.telegraph.co.uk/finance/businessclub/8010710/Do-women-fear-rejection-more-than-men.html

5. *Telegraph*: http://www.telegraph.co.uk/news/worldnews/
    asia/china/10484993/Why-Chinas-boom-may-be-coming-
    to-an-end-and-the-50-million-women-shortage-is-to-blame.
    html

6. http://harvardkennedyschoolreview.com/rwanda-strides-
    towards-gender-equality-in-government

7. https://www.execpipeline.com/research/women-
    count-2017/

8. http://www.execpipeline.com/research/women-count-2017

9. *Metro*: http://metro.co.uk/2017/07/19/bbc-salaries-report-
    reveals-women-are-paid-four-times-less-with-claudia-
    winkleman-the-highest-earning-female-star-6790566

10. *Independent*: https://www.independent.co.uk/news/uk/
    home-news/bbc-pay-private-school-highest-paid-half-stars-
    salaries-breakdown-a7854491.html;

11. *Guardian*: https://www.theguardian.com/commentisfree/
    2017/aug/07/restrict-privately-educated-britains-elite-quota;
    https://www.theguardian.com/media/2017/jul/19/bbc-salary-
    data-shows-huge-pay-gap-between-white-and-bme-stars

12. *Fortune*: http://www.fortune.com/2017/07/31/serena-
    williams-black-women-equal-pay/

13. *Fawcett Society*: https://www.fawcettsociety.org.uk/news/
    minority-ethnic-women-left-behind-pay-gap-progress

14. Yann Borgstedt's TEDx Talk: https://www.youtube.com/
    watch?v=4gpW9haB5nE

15. http://cwhf.org/inductees/politics-government-law/Clare-
    boothe-luce#.WwHZ3YXoDB8